Genre Realistic Fiction

Essential Question
How do people uncover what they have in common?

Treasures from Tonga

by
Melanie Drewery

illustrated by
Bradley Clark

Chapter 1 All Wrong 'Ofa

After my first day of school in America, I'm **miserable**. I want to go back to Tonga, my Pacific island home. I don't understand how things work here, and I feel as if I'm doing everything wrong.

I listen to my brother and sister **chattering** about their day. School is easy for my brother, Tevita. He's 15 and **fabulous** at sports. Because he's so good, he has made friends with the other boys who are only interested in sports. And when you're only seven, like my sister Alisi, everything is simple. Being my age, 12, is more complicated.

My mother, Sela, asks about my day. I try to smile, and I just say, "My new school is so enormous." I don't tell her how I was scared of getting lost. I don't say that nobody else was wearing a white button-up top and blue skirt like I was.

My father, James, arrives home from work. He asks about my day, and I remember something important. "I have to bring a present to school tomorrow," I say. I explain that the teacher called out everyone's name at the beginning of class. The others all said "Present" when the teacher said their names. I didn't have a present so I said "no," and everyone laughed.

"They didn't mean a present to give," James says, smiling kindly. "Present also means 'I'm here.'" I feel silly but also **relieved**. I'm less worried now that I don't have to bring a present. "Was there anything else you didn't understand?" James asks.

I tell him that no one else took off their shoes before going into the classroom. And nobody brought chicken and sweet potatoes for lunch.

James nods, and I can tell he understands. "I know this is a huge **adjustment** for you," he says, "but I think you will get used to it quickly."

"My friends said that I shouldn't call you James and Sela," Alisi adds. "They said I should call you Mom and Dad instead."

"Well, my name isn't Mom," Sela says, laughing, "so please don't call me that! 'Ofa, did you make any friends?"

"No," I say. "Maybe tomorrow."

"That's a good attitude," James says. "You might decide to lead a **nomadic** life someday and travel all over the world. Knowing how to make new friends will help."

"Tomorrow I'll put your chicken and kumala inside a sandwich so you'll feel more comfortable," Sela offers. I start to feel a little better.

STOP AND CHECK

Why is 'Ofa the only one who has trouble fitting in at school?

Chapter 2 Fitting In

The next day, I'm determined to fit in at school. I'll do whatever I need to do. I even hide a T-shirt in my bag. I also bring some bookmarks made out of tapa cloth, which is special in Tonga. Maybe I'll meet some kids who like to read as much as I do.

As soon as I get to school, I go to the girls' bathroom to change into my light-blue T-shirt. I undo my braids and start brushing my hair. Ashleigh and Katelyn, two girls from my class, come into the bathroom. They say that my hair looks amazing. I'm starting to fit in already.

Ashleigh and Katelyn walk with me to class. I'm trying to remember to say "yes" when Mr. Coleman calls my name, but I make another mistake. I forget to speak English, so I say "*'io.*"

"No again?" Mr. Coleman says, and everyone laughs.

I'm so **embarrassed** that my shame feels like a small **ember** is burning inside me.

But then someone helps me out. “She didn’t say ‘no,’ Mr. Coleman,” a girl named Emily says.

Mr. Coleman apologizes and asks what I said. I explain that I said “‘*io*,” which means “yes” in the Tongan language.

“That’s wonderful,” Mr. Coleman says. “It’s good to learn about other cultures. In fact, our next project is to learn about another country.”

I hear Ashleigh whisper to Katelyn, “We should do Tonga with ‘Ofa. Then we won’t have to research very much.”

I’d rather learn about a different country, but I want Ashleigh and Katelyn to like me. So I don’t say anything.

Later that day, the class goes to the library. Ashleigh asks if Tonga is like Hawaii. She wants to know if people in Tonga dance the hula or wear bikini tops made out of coconut shells.

"No, Tonga is a different country," I say. "We have our own dances and customs. We also have tapa cloth, which is very **sturdy**. I have some bookmarks made out of tapa." I take out the bookmarks and offer them to the kids around me. So many kids take bookmarks that Emily doesn't get one. I'm sorry, since she helped me that morning.

The librarian, Miss Tait, comes over to meet me. She explains how to check out books, and I ask how many books I can check out at once.

"You're a bookworm," Miss Tait says with a smile. It seems mean to call me a worm. Still, she looks nice, so I smile back.

STOP AND CHECK

Why is 'Ofa confused in the library?

Chapter 3 Doing What's Right

After school I change back into my white blouse and braid my hair. I find Alisi, and we sit outside. We wait for Tevita so we can all walk home together.

I see a woman and a small white dog by the fence. The dog looks so tiny standing in the middle of so many people. I feel as tiny as the dog. I feel so small because everything is so different from Tonga.

A girl walks up to the woman and the dog. I can tell that the dog is **overjoyed** when it **reunites** with its owner. It is so happy that it runs in circles. The girl turns around, and I see that it's Emily.

"That girl is in my class," I tell Alisi. "Let's ask if we can pet her dog."

Emily is happy that we like her dog, Pip.

While Alisi pets Pip, I tell Emily and her mother about the animals in Tonga. I explain that cats, chickens, pigs, and dogs always run around on the roads.

Then I notice that Emily is holding a book about Tonga. “Are you interested in Tonga?” I ask her.

She **blushes**, and her cheeks turn bright pink. “I want to travel there,” she says. “The book says that there are a lot of cool fish in Tonga. Is that true?”

“Yes, Tonga has colorful reef fish. There are sea snakes and humpback whales, too.”

“Wouldn’t it be amazing to swim with whales?” Emily says.

Emily’s mom says, “Yes, and I hope we do someday. But right now, it’s time to swim in the pool.”

Emily and her mom wave good-bye as they walk away with Pip pulling at the leash.

When Tevita finally comes out of the school, he tells us that he wants to walk home with his friends. He says, "It's not cool to walk with your sisters."

"Why would it be colder to walk with those guys?" Alisi asks, and Tevita's friends laugh.

I pull Alisi away and glare at Tevita because he's being rude. "Cool can also mean interesting or fun," I explain to Alisi.

I think about Emily on the way home. I'd like to work on the project with her because we have a good **rapport**. I think Emily and I would have fun together, but I don't want to offend Ashleigh and Katelyn. Then I think about how Tevita acted with his friends. He had changed.

I want friends who like me the way I am.

STOP AND CHECK

Why does 'Ofa want to work on the project with Emily?

Chapter 4 True Friends

The next day, I decide to wear my white blouse to school and keep my hair in braids.

I say "hi" to Ashleigh and Katelyn, but I sit next to Emily. I ask if she wants to be partners for the project.

"That would be great," she says, smiling, "but I wasn't planning to do the project on Tonga. I want to research Antarctica."

"That's awesome!" I say. "Did you know that the whales in Tonga swim up from Antarctica?"

"Yes, I've read that," she says. "I'm kind of a bookworm."

"That's what Miss Tait called me yesterday. I didn't understand what she meant," I say.

"A bookworm is someone who loves to read," Emily explains.

"Then I'm definitely a bookworm," I say. Emily and I smile at each other, and I know that I've found the right friend.

Emily and I sit next to each other at lunch. I see something strange in her lunchbox, so I ask what it is.

"Lasagna," she says, making a face. "It's what we had for dinner last night. I always get **leftovers** for lunch."

"I have leftovers, too!" I say. "But I asked Sela—I mean, my mom—to put them in sandwiches so I would fit in."

Emily says she might ask her mom to do the same, and then we share our lunches. I think the lasagna is delicious, and Emily likes the kumala.

We go to the library when we're done eating. Emily is helping Miss Tait make a **display** that shows about different cultures. She explains that Miss Tait is her **mentor**. Miss Tait asks me to help with the display. She says sharing my culture is like sharing a treasure.

STOP AND CHECK

What fact do both 'Ofa and Emily already know about Antarctica?

TONGA

After school Alisi and I walk home with Emily, her mother, and Pip.

"'Ofa is bringing some treasures from Tonga for the library display," Emily tells her mother. "We're going to show everyone how different life is in the Pacific."

Emily's mother suggests that we also think about the things that are the same. "People understand each other's cultures better when they find things in common," she says.

Emily and I talk about all the things we have in common. We both like reading and whales and swimming. And we both like Pip!

Emily asks her mother if I can go to the pool with them tomorrow. She says I can as long as my parents agree.

"What else do you have in common?" Alisi wonders.

Emily and I look at each other, and then we burst out laughing.

"Leftovers for lunch!" we say loudly.

"What's wrong with leftovers?" Emily's mother says with a grin.

"Nothing," I say. "Nothing at all."

STOP AND CHECK

What do 'Ofa and Emily have in common?

Respond to Reading

Summarize

Summarize *Treasures from Tonga*. Use important details from the story. Your graphic organizer may help you.

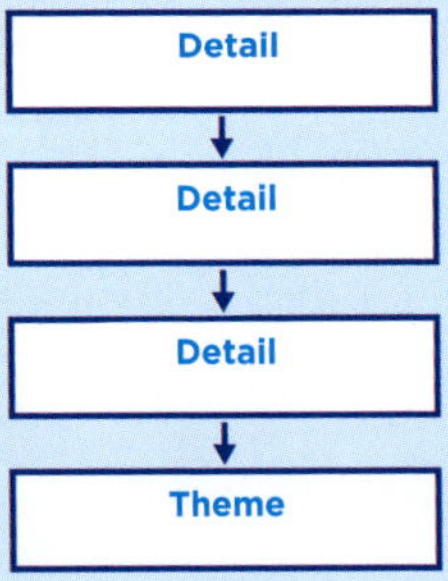

Text Evidence

1. What is the theme of this story? Find a detail in the story that supports your answer. **THEME**
2. Find the word *determined* on page 5. What clues help you to understand the word's meaning? **VOCABULARY**
3. Write about how 'Ofa's feelings change during the story. How does this change show the story's theme? **WRITE ABOUT READING**

Genre Realistic Fiction

Compare Texts

Read about how a boy from Africa finds something in common with people in America.

Bigger, LOUDER, Faster

The glass doors slide, I am pushed through by over-tall people and suitcases rolling like cattle hooves on a dry road to the other side.

I am Paco, the son, far from Botswana. The hard gray ground accepts my feet. No African dust to soften my steps as I search for Ntate, my father. He will meet me here in America, a land unlike my own.

We drive in a stream of too-big trucks and cars dashing, growling like wild dogs with paws of rubber in a twisting traffic chain wider than the Limpopo River.

"Relax," says Ntate, "enjoy the sights."

These sights are pasted on billboards big as buses crowding the roadsides and my eyes.

My ears catch a thin siren calling, in chords of chaos, a strange greeting, welcome welcome welcome. I laugh. "I am happy to see you, too," says Ntate.

Sleep leans on my window as I watch the sky's skin stretching over huge hills, houses clinging to their sides like ticks on cattle flanks. My mouth is an open cave of surprise.

"It is all big and loud and fast here," I say in my new room, bigger than a house in Botswana. "Not everything," says Ntate. "Some things are the same." Across the street, there is a dog like mine, and children.

Ntate gives me a ball. The children call out "Hello," their dog leaps after my ball, and we run laughing. This friendship is just the right size.

Make Connections

What helps the boy in *Bigger, Louder, Faster* feel more at home in his new country? **ESSENTIAL QUESTION**

How do books in *Treasures from Tonga* and a ball in *Bigger, Louder, Faster* help the main characters make new friends? **TEXT TO TEXT**

Focus on Literary Elements

Foreshadowing Writers often give their readers clues about what might happen later in the story. This is called foreshadowing. It helps to keep readers interested.

Read and Find The author show us that 'Ofa is having a hard time adjusting to life in America. 'Ofa has several problems during the story. Each problem foreshadows the solution. On page 6, Emily helps 'Ofa out at roll call. This is foreshadowing. It gives a hint that Emily might be the friend that 'Ofa needs.

Your Turn

Work with a partner. Reread the story. Look for other clues that foreshadow how 'Ofa's problems might be solved.

Discuss how the foreshadowing helped you guess what would happen.